Stones and Stories

Stones and Stories

A Primer on Literary Analysis,
Hermeneutics, and Writing

JUDITH E. ANDERSON

RESOURCE *Publications* · Eugene, Oregon

STONES AND STORIES
A Primer on Literary Analysis, Hermeneutics, and Writing

Resource Publications
An Imprint of Wipf and Stock Publishers
199 W. 8th Ave., Suite 3
Eugene, OR 97401

www.wipfandstock.com

PAPERBACK ISBN: 978-1-5326-7388-7
HARDCOVER ISBN: 978-1-5326-7389-4
EBOOK ISBN: 978-1-5326-7390-0

Manufactured in the U.S.A.   FEBRUARY 15, 2019

For Joshua

"For it is no empty word for you, but your very life, and by this word you shall live long in the land that you are going over the Jordan to possess."

Deuteronomy 32:47

Contents

Permissions

Preface

MAELSTROM WAS ONE OF the many unfamiliar words I encountered while reading E. A. Poe's stories as a young person. Its foreignness filled it with an emotional transport that its familiar synonym *whirlpool* lacked. I recognized at some level that though these words were similar in their denotations, they differed wildly in their connotations.

My early interest in reading and language took time to develop. It was my conversion to faith in Christ in my early twenties and my consequential career teaching high school English in a public school that brought bloom to that dormant seed. My conversion affected my mind and heart in several ways. Lazy and indifferent during high school, I now understood that people and things mattered, and that life had meaning. The strong teaching and preaching in the church I joined fed my new hunger for theology. This led to a hunger for stories from literature, history, philosophy, and science. I wanted to understand how human knowledge reflects and rebels against the God who is wisdom, understanding, knowledge, and righteousness.[1]

Stories is one of those words that has differing denotations *and* connotations. A fairy tale is a story. The account of a person's life is a story. An outright lie may also be referred to as a story. So the denotations of the word include truth, falsehood, and some mixture of the two. Ambiguity of this kind frustrated some of my high school students. A few determined that non-fictional stories

---

1. See Isa 11: 1–5 and 1 Cor 1:18–31 for instance.

were more trustworthy vehicles of truth and knowledge than fictional stories were. This seems credible at first glance, but one objective in our teaching of critical thinking was to show students that truth and falsehood can be found in both kinds of stories. Besides the obvious dilemma of which methodologies are used to assess the finer points of a term such as *truth*, a problem sometimes resulted when students uncritically replaced the error of their earlier simplistic ideas with the error of newly acquired sophisticated ideas. For instance, as they grew to recognize the operation of a subjective point of view in their literary analysis, some were quick to adopt a philosophical position, (supported by the cultural milieu) that nullified the desirability or possibility of an absolute.

The literary works we studied encouraged, disputed, and modified this relativistic claim. I hope students learned how to discern an author's belief system as they discussed and wrote about key themes throughout their high school career. I enjoyed teaching them that there are many different lenses through which we can view life and literature—pantheism, feminism, Freudianism, and Christianity among them—but I felt stifled by constraints against teaching as truth the doctrines of Scripture.

This primer, *Stones and Stories*, was born out of my curtailed freedom. It began as a small set of exercises on figurative language in Scripture that I intended to share with my grandson. Based on the question "What do these stones mean?" found in the Book of Joshua, it grew into a broader examination of the principles of interpretation. From there it expanded further into the purposes and practice of writing.

Despite this expansion, *Stones and Stories* remains a primer. As an introductory text, it necessarily excludes weightier material in each of the three categories of its subtitle—literary analysis, hermeneutics, and writing. It aims to introduce or reinforce a framework of principles in each of these disciplines while grounding these basic precepts in practical exercises supplemented by extensive footnotes.

Stones and Stories is a blend of textbook, study guide, journal, and reference work formats, making it adaptable to several learning and discussion settings. Though chiefly written for high school students in public, private, or home schooling environments, it might also serve as a text for youth groups and Sunday schools. It is designed for individual reflection and response, but it also invites group discussion. Parts of this book might spark meaningful discussion during family devotions.

Academic study should not be at odds with Christian discipleship. Understood rightly, academic study is one of many God-given tasks that the disciple undertakes to serve and glorify the LORD "who teaches man knowledge."[2] This knowledge begins with an awareness of our utter moral defenselessness before a Holy God.[3] It graciously includes the assurance that God has provided his people with a means of atonement.[4] It makes genuine education and good works possible for his disciples as they submit to his word: "All Scripture is breathed out by God and profitable for teaching, for reproof, for correction, and for training in righteousness, that the man of God may be complete, equipped for every good work."[5] Scripture primes us for all of our knowledge pursuits, not that we might become proud, but that we might enjoy God abundantly—and that he might receive the glory due his holy name.

2. Ps 94:10.

3. "through the law comes knowledge of sin" Rom. 3:20b.

4. "to give knowledge of salvation to his people / in the forgiveness of their sins" (Luke 1:77).

5. 2 Tim 3:16.

Acknowledgments

It is never trite to acknowledge that God is to receive all glory for anything of perceived good in our works: SDG. In his great abundance, God has blessed me with many teachers and encouragers—in my life and in my writing. Among these are my husband, Donald, and other family members; the pastors, elders, Sunday school teachers, Bible study leaders and friends of my Church family; and even a few others who I hope will one day be part of Christ's sheepfold. My gratitude also to the editors of Wipf and Stock for their encouragement and expertise.

Introduction

Literary Analysis, Hermeneutics, and Writing

LITERATURE IS INEXTRICABLY LINKED to life. Its origins and its subjects are found in life. The particular piece of literature around which *Stones and Stories* is centered—the Bible—*is* life. Like other literature, the Bible offers life for the mind, life for the heart, and life for the body as we travel this earthly terrain. Unlike other literature, the Bible offers life eternal—a life beyond the Jordan and eternal meaning for the lives we live on this earth.

This distinction is so crucial that it may seem *scandalous* to apply the vocabulary, techniques, and practice of literary analysis to our reading of sacred Scripture. But this kind of sharp division between the sacred and the secular ignores one astounding reality of the Incarnation. The omnipotent God, who spoke the universe into being, the holy God, who revealed the chasm separating him from his fallen creation, stooped to our experience when he sent his Son into our world. Jesus, the Word made flesh, knowingly made himself vulnerable to misunderstanding, humiliation, and worse.

This gives us pause. Aware of our propensity to err, we might think it best to avoid Scriptural analysis or interpretation. It seems a scandalous activity—this is the very word of God! We are right to fear. The word *scandal* comes from a Greek word meaning "stumbling block, a cause of moral stumbling."[1] If we misuse Scripture in our conversations with unbelievers, then we have "put a stumbling block before the blind"[2] and have not loved our neighbor as ourselves. If we read Scripture to suit our individual preferences, we grievously offend God. Peter learns this. When he rebukes[3] Jesus because Jesus's teaching does not accord with his preferences, Jesus replies, "Get behind me, Satan! You are a stumbling block to me; you do not have in mind the things of God, but the things of men."[4] These passages should not dissuade us from analysis, however. They implicitly teach that analysis and interpretation are necessary so that we may avoid scandalous error. Because our intellects—like our wills, emotions, bodies, and whole beings—are fallen, we cannot do this perfectly. But God has provided his Church with his Holy Spirit; with pastors, missionaries, and teachers; and with many written and spoken resources to help us understand the "things of God" found in his Word. This should encourage us to study this Word, humbly grateful to God that the scandal of the cross is no longer a stumbling block to our own formerly blind and worldly minds and hearts,[5] and dependent upon him to grow the love for him and others that excels "all mysteries and all knowledge."[6]

The roots of the word *hermeneutics*, which is defined as the methods used in interpretation, include reference to the Greek god Hermes.[7] Hermes, according to mythology, presided over a vast and disparate[8] set of human activities; among these was rhetorically excellent speech and writing. Perhaps we all aspire to clear, convincing eloquence in our discourse. Certainly we are drawn to

1. Hoad, *The Concise Oxford Dictionary of English Etymology*, 420.

2. Lev 19:14.

3. This one word reveals the perversity of Peter's error.

4. Matt 16:23 NIV.

5. 1 Cor 1:18–25.

6. 1 Cor 13:2.

7. Moules, "Hermetic Inquiry," 2.

8. *disparate* means different and not comparable. It is not to be confused with the word *desperate* which means hopeless.

those song lyrics, stirring speeches, and verses of poetry that combine beauty of expression with clarity of thought and feeling. How interesting, then, that the God of Scripture calls the ineloquent and slow of speech Moses[9] to lead his people out of slavery, and the unskilled speaker Paul[10] to build Christ's Church in number and in doctrinal depth. These examples do not negate the power of elegant speech and writing; indeed, homage to Scriptural eloquence has been paid by Biblical scholars and secular authors alike. Instead, they teach us that the wisdom of God is not hindered by human inadequacy nor made accessible by human eloquence. It is "the Spirit who is from God," who helps us in "interpreting spiritual truths."[11]

Truth has been under assault ever since the serpent entered Eden. Perhaps its most well-known derision came from the lips of Pontius Pilate. Standing in a quintessentially ironic position of judgment against Jesus, the Son of God who *is* truth, Pilate questioned the very *idea* of truth.[12] Then, as the crowd clamored for Jesus's death, Pilate "brought Jesus out and sat down on the judgment seat at a place called The Stone Pavement."[13] Shortly thereafter, he delivered Jesus over to be crucified. The goal of *Stones and Stories*, then, is to help students of literature and life see that the Book about the Word who is "the way, the truth, and the life" promises to teach us how not to "judge by appearances, but judge with right judgment."[14]

9. Exod 4:10.

10. 2 Cor 11:6.

11. 1 Cor 2:12–13.

12. John 18:38.

13. John 19:13.

14. John 7:24.

1

"What Do These Stones Mean?"[1]

CHILDREN ASKED THEIR PARENTS this question when they saw
the twelve stones set up at Gilgal by the side of the Jordan River.
The stones had obviously been arranged. They were not naturally
gathered together, so it was logical (and expected) that someone
seeing the stones would wonder about their significance. When
the children asked, they would be told the story.

Stones and stories share an integral connection. Stories are
built from elements or parts, just as walls, monuments, bridges,
and houses are built from stones. When we read a story, we pay
attention to the characters, places, and events that build the story.
We also wonder what the story means. Like the twelve stones set
up in Gilgal, the people, places and events of stories are arranged
in a way that tells a story and points to some kind of meaning.

MODES OF WRITING

Writing that tells a story is just one of four kinds (or modes) of
writing. Each mode is built with words and ideas. The finished
piece of writing is the completed structure; the words and ideas

1. Josh 4:21.

may be thought of as the stones with which the structure is built. Here are the names given to the four kinds of written discourse:[2]

- *Narrative Mode*: In this mode, writers use words to build setting, character, plot, and theme. These elements are arranged to present a story, just as masons and sculptors use stones to build walls, buildings, and memorials.

- *Persuasive Mode*: Writers also use words to build arguments. An argument in this sense is not a quarrel. It is a reasoned statement about a contested topic that seeks to persuade readers to understand and agree with the writer's stance. Persuasive writing depends upon the elements (facts, histories, logic) of the argument, the arrangement of these elements, and the language (diction, tone, and figures of speech[3]) used to express the arguments. These elements, arrangements, and word choices are similar to the stones and process a builder uses.

- *Descriptive Mode*: As the name suggests, descriptive writing is built with words that illustrate an object, place, or idea. The object being described may be extraordinary or ordinary, unique or universal. Effective descriptions of the unfamiliar require comparison to something that is familiar. Effective descriptions of the ordinary require fresh comparisons to help the reader see the familiar object in a new light. Descriptive writing is built with the stones of ideas and words chosen for their sensory power and their connotations.[4]

- *Expositional Mode*: The expositional writer explains (exposits, expounds upon) or offers information about some topic. An essay about the making, transporting, and arrangement

2. Some will insist upon more categories, but these suffice.

3. *Diction* is word choice. *Tone* is the emotional aspect of the word choice. *Figures of speech* are words not intended in a literal sense.

4. *Sensory language* refers to words that appeal to the five senses: sight, sound, taste, touch and smell. Sensory language is also called *imagery*. *Connotation* refers to the associations a word suggests. *Connotation* differs from *denotation*, which means the dictionary definition of a word.

of the stones used in constructing pyramids is one example of exposition. Exposition can take several forms. It may, for instance, explain the *classifications* of tools and procedures used by pyramid builders. It may explain the *process* of building pyramids. It may *compare* and *contrast* different kinds of pyramids.

Exercise: **Drawing a Chart**—Chart the persuasive, descriptive, and expositional modes of discourse, labeling the stones that serve as elements or foundations of each particular writing mode. A sample chart of the narrative mode follows:

The *story* suggests a theme or themes, the "what does it mean" question. *Theme* is a statement of meaning that the reader deduces from the story's elements. More than just a topic (such as courage or suffering), a theme says something about the thematic topic ("courage is sometimes quiet," or "suffering takes many forms" etc.).

Motif a recurring image, idea, or word with connotative or symbolic significance. In repeating throughout the story, motifs help develop the story's theme.

FOUNDATION STONE: words describing the *setting* ("washed in sunlight," "cluttered with memories")

FOUNDATION STONE: words that create *characters* (e.g. "wizened," "carefree," "bold," "thoughtful")

FOUNDATION STONE: words describing *conflict* ("the whipping power of a hurricane," "the seething anger of envy")

Some writing combines modes, and not all writing fits neatly into these four categories. Informational texts such as dictionaries, encyclopedias, and instruction manuals lack narrative, persuasive, or descriptive purpose, and are usually categorized as expository writing. This kind of expository writing might be compared to a stone wall that only serves to show where someone's property ends:

Perhaps you're thinking, "Yes, but some boundary walls have a story behind them. There's more to the wall's existence than the mere marking of property divisions." You're very perceptive! The stories lodged in some boundary walls may not be evident. In a similar vein, the meanings of some stories are not readily apparent. They may be implicit rather than explicit.[5] Other stone works, like other kinds of writing, have an explicit story to tell. Powerful examples include the Wailing Wall (also referred to as the Western Wall) in Jerusalem and the Martin Luther King Jr. Memorial in Washington, DC. Find photos online of these two monuments. Write a few sentences about what these stones mean. (Big hint: The MLK Jr. Memorial is named "The Stone of Hope" from Dr. King's famous "I Have a Dream" speech.)

FICTION AND NON-FICTION

We have categorized different kinds of writing according to their purposes and methods: narrative, persuasive, descriptive, or expository. Another category classifies writing according to a definition of factual truth. This classification identifies a book as fiction or non-fiction.

---

5. *Explicit* means clearly or overtly stated. *Implicit* (*imply* is the verb form) means suggested or indicated but not stated outright. Note: *imply* and *insinuate* differ in that *insinuate* suggests an accusatory implication.

A common but *not* very accurate definition of fiction and non-fiction follows: Fiction is not true or real, and non-fiction is true or real. One reason this is not an accurate definition is that fiction, which is constructed mainly of imagined characters, places, and plots, often teaches something true and real. On the other hand, a work of non-fiction such as a history of a conflict or a biography of a famous sports figure might not give a fully accurate account. The author may choose and arrange the facts about the conflict or athlete so as to present a limited point of view. One account of a battle might favor one side while another account favors the other side, yet both are catalogued as non-fiction. Different biographies about the same person may present opposing impressions, yet both are termed non-fiction. Even if authors do not intentionally skew their accounts, they are limited by their bias[6] and by their inability to know all there is to know about the history or the person they're writing about.

Fiction often teaches us truths, even if its characters, setting, and plot are a product of the author's imagination. For example, *The Lion, the Witch, and the Wardrobe* is classified as fiction, but it tells of real and true grief over the death of a loved one. Some fiction, such as *The Scarlet Letter,* is overtly connected to biographical and historical facts. Even so, it is a work of imagination. A better definition of fiction might be this: fiction is a story that has characters, plot, and a setting that are imagined by the story's author. Examples of fiction include novels and short stories.

Non-Fiction does not imagine the characters, setting, or plot of the book. The details of the biography or history are usually factual, but the meaning created by the author's arrangement of facts and research is to some extent inadequate or even distorted. A better definition of non-fiction might be this: Non-fiction is writing that gives an account of a person(s), event(s), or idea(s), based upon factual research conducted by the author. Examples

---

6. *Bias* is usually understood as an undesirable and sometimes correctable perspective. I use the term here to indicate the system of ideas—not necessarily or always wrongheaded—that one has of the world.

of non-fiction include biographies and autobiographies, histories, some essays, and some forms of journalism.

The Bible, a word traceable through several languages, means "books."[7] It is obviously literature. It is also *sui generis*, a Latin term meaning that it is in a category of its own. It is neither fiction nor non-fiction, though it makes use of imagined stories and of historical facts. For instance, Jesus told stories known as parables. The characters, plots and settings of these parables may not be literally true, but the meanings of these parables are certainly true. We also find descriptions in the Bible that are literally true. Records of persons, places, conflicts, cultural practices, and geographical peculiarities are examples of this sort. But the Bible does not just offer information, and it cannot be classified as non-fiction or fiction. It makes use of many genres and modes of writing, but it refuses categorization. Its assortment of genres is not sufficient reason to grant it *sui generis* status, however, especially in today's mashup, genre-busting literary practice. It is its author and authority that set the Bible apart as one of a kind.

Some people will agree that the Bible has wonderful narratives, jaw-dropping descriptions, powerful arguments, and thoughtful expositions. But they attribute these writings to human authors who were merely products of their epochs and cultures. The epochs and cultures represented by the writers of these sixty-six books, however, are vast and diverse; yet the Bible as a whole is unified and cohesive. Its human writers themselves insist that their spoken and written words are not their own. The Old Testament authors consistently attribute their words to the LORD. New Testament writers continue in this vein. The Apostle Paul, for instance, commends the Greek believers at Thessalonica because "when you received the word of God, which you heard from us, you accepted it not as the word of men but as what it really is, the word of God."[8] The writer of the Book of Acts commends the Jewish believers in Berea because they "received the word with all eagerness, examining the Scriptures daily to see if these things were

7. Hoad, *Concise Oxford*, 40.
8. 1 Thess 2:13.

so."[9] The Apostle Peter, reminding his audience that he and others were eyewitnesses of Christ's majesty and hearers of God's voice, exults in the reality that "we have the prophetic word more fully confirmed . . . knowing this first of all, that no prophecy of Scripture comes from someone's own interpretation. For no prophecy was ever produced by the will of man, but men spoke from God as they were carried along by the Holy Spirit."[10]

This is a bedrock[11] truth in our study of the stones and stories of Scripture.

9. Acts 17:11.
10. 2 Pet 1:19–21.
11. pun intended

2

What Do These Words Mean?

Figurative Language (Figures of Speech): Hyperbole, Metaphor, Simile, Personification, and Symbol

NEARLY ALL LITERARY WRITERS make use of figurative language, whether writing in a narrative, persuasive, descriptive, or expository mode. When an author chooses words that are not meant literally or factually, the author is using *figures of speech*, which are also referred to as *figurative language*. Figures of speech take different forms. Examples of figures of speech include *hyperbole, metaphor, simile, personification,* and *symbol*. There are many others as well.

- *Hyperbole*: The statement, "I am so hungry I could eat a horse,"[1] is not literally (actually) true or factual. No one could eat an entire horse in one meal (even if he wanted to). The statement is exaggerated to show that the person is *very* hungry. This kind of figurative language is called *hyperbole*

---

1. American writers place periods and commas inside the end quote marks. British writers reverse this style.

(hi-*purr*-bow-lee), a Greek word similar in meaning to the English word, "exaggeration."[2]

- *Metaphor*: The word *metaphor* (*met*-a-for) also comes from the Greek language and means "to transfer."[3] It too is a figure of speech, meaning that it is not meant to be understood literally. The statement, "She is a rock" is not meant literally. This woman is compared to a rock because a rock is strong or unmovable. These rock qualities are transferred to the woman by means of this metaphor.

- *Simile*: (*sim*-i-lee) is a word of Latin origin meaning "similar or like."[4] Like a metaphor, a simile compares different entities. Unlike a metaphor, it uses *like* or *as* in making this comparison. The statement, "He has been like a rock to me" compares the man to a rock because of the same qualities of strength and immovability foundational to the metaphor above, but because it compares the two by using *like*, we call this figure of speech a simile.

- *Personification* (purr-sonn-i-fi-*cay*-shun) is a term of French origin meaning "represent" or "embodiment."[5] It does what it sounds like it might do: it assigns characteristics of *person*hood to things that are not persons. Whenever we talk about trees clapping or skies smiling, we are using personification. Animated movies are often full of personification. This is because *animated* means something similar to *personified*.

- *Symbol*: is another term of Latin origin meaning "mark, token, outward sign."[6] At the most fundamental level, every word in a language is a symbol since it is a "token" of the idea or entity it represents. The word *eye* is not an eye, it is a symbol for an eye. Some words have another layer of "outward

2. Trumble, Brown, *Shorter Oxford English*, 1299.
3. Hoad, *Concise Oxford*, 291.
4. Trumble, Brown, *Shorter Oxford English*, 2840.
5. American Heritage, 4th ed., NY: Houghton Mifflin, 1039.
6. Trumble, Brown, *Shorter Oxford English*, 3148.

sign[age]." These literary symbols are words (e.g.[7] *cold* or *hand*) or even just a letter, such as Nathaniel Hawthorne's A, that have literal significance but always suggest other important interpretative meanings as well. For instance, *cold* may refer to the measurable temperature of a house, but it may also symbolize the emotional affect[8] of the people who live in that house.

A BIT MORE ABOUT SYMBOLISM

Many literary symbols are drawn from familiar physical entities such as eyes, birds, trees, hands, and mountains. These physical or natural (i.e.,[9] found in nature) elements are associated with ideas, emotions, or other abstract concepts that are more difficult to understand because they are intangible.[10] For example, eyes (eyes are tangible) commonly symbolize a person's soul (a soul is intangible). Hands (tangible) often symbolize the motive (intangible) or consequences of a person's actions.

Understanding symbolism is complicated (in a way that writers and some readers find delightful) by the multiplicity of possible associations inherent in symbology. Birds, for instance, offer a disparate variety of symbolic associations. Depending upon the species and the culture, they might symbolize freedom, memory, wisdom, love, evil, peace, war, rebirth, or death.

Abstract realities (such as souls, motives, wisdom, and freedom) are important to our understanding of ourselves and the

7. e.g. is an abbreviation of the Latin phrase *exempli gratia* (for the purpose of example). It means, "for example."

8. This is one of the few instances where the word *affect* is not a verb. *Affect* and *effect* are frequently confused. While *affect* is usually a verb meaning "to influence," it is used here as a noun that identifies an emotional state or condition. *Effect* is usually (but not always) a noun meaning "result." As a verb, *effect* means "to bring about change."

9. i.e. is an abbreviation of the Latin *id est* (that is). It means, "in other words."

10. *intangible* means not material or not able to be touched.

world outside ourselves. Because they are abstract, they cannot be understood through our senses—our ability to see, taste, touch, smell, or hear. We can, however, understand something about some abstract realities through their comparisons to those phenomena we know through our senses. For instance, light is used throughout Scripture to symbolize God's presence, truth, and goodness. It's often explicitly or implicitly paired with its opposite, darkness. Darkness commonly symbolizes abandonment, ignorance, and evil.

The stones at Gilgal are another symbol. They are tangible—able to be seen and touched—and they point to an abstract concept(s) about God. If you have not already done so, read Joshua 4 to see if you can determine the abstract concept(s) that the stones are arranged to teach and to remember.

A BIT MORE ABOUT FIGURES OF SPEECH

Like the *symbol*, each figurative image—*hyperbole*, *metaphor*, *simile*, and *personification*—creates an interesting impression that a literal statement lacks. The literal statements "I am really hungry," "She is emotionally strong," and "I have always been able to depend upon him" may communicate something true, but they lack the mental and emotional impact of their figurative counterparts.[11] This is one reason why writers work with figures of speech. They want to tap the power that words have to show us the iceberg of meaning beneath the piece of ice floating visibly on the surface.

NB:[12] Many shortcuts end in being lost. If you decide that any sentence that contains *like* is a simile, you will often be mistaken. For instance, in Revelation, we read,

---

11. When figures of speech are used too often, they become *clichés*. Though "I am so hungry I could eat a horse," "She is a rock," and "He is like a rock" serve as examples of hyperbole, metaphor, and simile, each one of these statements has become clichéd because of overuse. Clichés indicate laziness or a lack of creativity. Strive for fresh figurative language.

12. NB: or n.b. (Latin for *nota bene*, which means "note well" or "pay attention").

Then a mighty angel took up a stone *like* [italics added] a great millstone and threw it into the sea, saying, "So will Babylon the great city be thrown down with violence, and will be found no more; / and the sound of harpists and musicians, of flute players and trumpeters, / will be heard in you no more." [13]

Why is "like a great millstone" not a simile? (If you have trouble answering this question, return to the definition of simile. What does a simile do exactly?)

Not every comparison between different entities is a simile or metaphor. Some comparisons, such as the one above, are more properly understood as analogies. The differences and definitions are not always clear-cut, but analogies usually compare two *sets* of entities. In the Revelation quotation, the first set consists of the action of the angel's violent throwing of a weighty millstone into a sea. This action is compared to the action of the second set, which is the violent throwing of Babylon into oblivion. Typically, the literal elements of an analogy (angel, millstone, sea) suggest a secondary symbolic meaning. In this instance, the millstone is explicitly linked to the symbolic Babylon. Not every analogue is revealed this explicitly.

IDENTIFYING FIGURES OF SPEECH

Stones make good building materials in architecture. We need good building materials to make stories, too. We can see a stone building, bridge, roadway, or pyramid; but we cannot "see" a story except in our minds. Figures of speech help create a visual picture.

TRY IT! #1

The following eight quotations use the word *stone(s)* in a figurative sense. Identify the figure(s) of speech in each quotation; then, analyze the effect of this figurative language by following the directions in the chart and example below. If the quotation contains more than one kind of figure of speech, write answers for each

13. Rev 18:21–22.

one. If the quotation contains more than one instance of the same kind of figure of speech, write answers for each instance. While there are "wrong answers" in literary analysis, there are often unexpected answers that open areas of deeper understanding.

Use the footnotes to look up each quotation for fuller context, but be sure to confine your answers to the given figure of speech. Example #8 is easier to answer if you understand the definition of *Ebenezer*, which is found in the footnotes of most Bibles.

	a)	b)	c)	d)
Simile or Metaphor	Underline: just the simile or metaphor	Write: *This is a simile.* OR: *This is a metaphor.*	Write: a sentence identifying the two entities being compared	Write: sentence(s) explaining what quality of the stone is emphasized in this comparison
Hyperbole	Underline: every word that is exaggerated	Write: *This is an example of hyperbole.* OR *This is hyperbolic.*	Write: a sentence stating what trait is being exaggerated	n/a
Personification	Underline: the trait or action that people (not stones) possess or perform	Write: *This is an example of personification.*	Write: a sentence identifying the personal trait or action given to the stone	Write: a sentence explaining the reason this stone is being personified
Symbol	Underline: the word that identifies what the stone stands for or symbolizes	Write: *This is a symbol.*	Write: a sentence identifying the abstract concept symbolized by the stone	Write: a sentence explaining why the stone is an apt symbol for the abstract concept

Example:

In the morning, when the wine had gone out of Nabal, his wife told him these things, and his heart died within him, and he became <u>as a stone</u> (a).[14]

b. This is a simile.

c. The two entities are *he* and *stone*. *Nabal* is compared to a *stone*.

d. This comparison shows the man's apparent lifelessness. A quality of stone is that it is non-living. The man was living, but when his heart failed him, he became as lifeless as a stone. (The next verse, interestingly, tells us that he actually died ten days later.)

1. "I tell you, if these were silent, the very stones would cry out."[15]

 b.

 c.

 d.

2. And the king made silver and gold as common in Jerusalem as stone.[16]

 b.

 c.

 d.

---

14. 1 Sam 25:37.
15. Luke 19:40.
16. 2 Chr 1:15.

3. Among all these were 700 chosen men who were left-handed; every one could sling a stone at a hair and not miss.[17]

    b.

    c.

    d.

4. Behold, this stone shall be a witness against us . . .[18]

    b.

    c.

    d.

5. . . . for [this stone] has heard all the words of the LORD that he spoke to us. [19]

    b.

    c.

    d.

6. I will give you a new heart, and a new spirit I will put within you. And I will remove the heart of stone from your flesh and give you a heart of flesh.[20]

    b.

    c.

    d.

17. Judg 20:16.
18. Josh 24:27.
19. Josh 24:27b.
20. Ezek 36:26.

7. And the LORD their God shall save them in that day as the flock of his people; for they shall be as the stones of a crown, lifted up as an ensign upon his land.[21]

   b.

   c.

   d.

8. Then Samuel took a stone and set it up between Mizpah and Shen and called its name Ebenezer; for he said, "Till now the LORD has helped us." [22]

   b.

   c.

   d.

---

21. Zech 9:16 (KJV). Though arguably analogic, what figurative examples are illustrated?

22. 1 Sam 7:12.

3

Context

"Text without Context Is Pretext"[1]

Stones are a frequent presence in the stories of many books of the Bible and of the story of the Bible as a whole. We find an important instance early in the Pentateuch, in Exodus. The Ten Commandments are written on tablets of stone by the finger of God ("finger" here is a figure of speech since God is Spirit and does not have fingers as we do[2]). We find another important instance at the end of the Bible, in the book of Revelation, where God's heavenly city is described as being adorned by many kinds of precious stones.

As we've seen, these stones are sometimes mentioned figuratively. When Nabal receives his wife's news, his heart dies within him, and "he became as a stone" though he did not die for about ten days. Perhaps he suffered a stroke. Perhaps he became catatonic. Whatever medical condition afflicted him in the days preceding his death, the stone simile aptly pictures his hard-heartedness and

---

1. Some quotations cannot be definitively linked to their author. The NY Public Library has a helpful site: https://www.nypl.org/blog/2013/11/22/how-to-research-quotations

2. This is also referred to in this instance as anthropomorphic language.

hard-headedness, the very traits that earn him his fate.[3] The figurative image, in this instance, communicates more truth than the mere mention of his immobility would. But a caveat[4] is necessary: although we are studying the figurative possibilities of stones, we must admit that sometimes stones are, well, just stones—and not much more than that.

TRY IT! #2

Read the following five quotations and decide whether the stone is just a stone or whether it suggests something more. Write your answer in this manner: if it is just a stone, write "literal stone." If you think it means something else as well, write "literal and figurative stone." (*Tip:* is anything being compared to anything else? If so, the author may be using the stone figuratively.) If *stone* is being used figuratively, write a sentence explaining the meaning of the comparison.

1. He dug it and cleared it of stones, / and planted it with choice vines;[5]

2. "Or which one of you, if his son asks him for bread, will give him a stone?"[6]

3. So David prevailed over the Philistine with a sling and with a stone,[7]

---

3. His name means "fool." See 1 Sam 25:25 and its note in ESV.
4. *caveat* (*caa*-vee-ott) a noun meaning warning or caution.
5. Isa 5:2.
6. Matt 7:9.
7. 1 Sam 17:50.

4. On that day I will make Jerusalem a heavy stone for all the peoples. All who lift it will surely hurt themselves.[8]

5. How the gold has grown dim, / how the pure gold is changed! / The holy stones lie scattered / at the head of every street.[9]

CONTEXT—THE SURROUNDING STORY

Maybe you thought that you needed more of the surrounding story to decide whether the stone referred to was "just a stone" or something with figurative potential. You're right! Let's look at the last example (#5 above) from Lamentations, a poetic work probably written by the prophet Jeremiah.

One kind of context is historical (the facts from history that surround the text). History teaches that the temple and all of Jerusalem had been destroyed by Nebuchadnezzar sometime before Lamentations was penned; Jeremiah's poetic book is a lament (an expression of grief) over this horrific event. Lamentations 4:1, then, seems to be a literal description of the ruined gold and scattered stones of the destroyed temple.

8. Zech 12:3. Though analogic, address the figurative element.

9. Lam 4:1. When quoting lines of poetry (Lamentations is a collection of poems), use forward slashes to indicate where the line breaks occur in the original poem. MLA and CMOS recommend that a four-line quotation like this be blocked (indented) as it is in the paragraph below, rather than written in the same line with slashes. I've transgressed the rule to illustrate the two styles of quoting verse.

Another kind of context is structural (the organization of the poem itself). Lam. 4:1 is followed by this verse:

> The precious sons of Zion,
>
> worth their weight in fine gold,
>
> how they are regarded as earthen pots,
>
> the work of a potter's hands!

Reading verse 1 together with verse 2, we discern a figurative as well as a literal interpretation of the verses. The structural context encourages a hermeneutic connection between the "holy stones" of verse 1 and the "precious sons of Zion" in verse 2.

Written Response #1: Write a brief (three to five sentence) paragraph[10] explaining (expository writing) the literal and figurative meanings of the "holy stones" in Lamentations 4:1. State the meanings in your first sentence if possible. Limit your explanation and evidence (specific word choices) to Lamentations 4:1–2. Consider the following questions in preparing your written response:

1. Why is the image of stones an effective figure of speech for the writer to use in this particular context? What qualities of stones (before and after temple's destruction) help him make the point he is making about the sons of Zion?

2. In addition to the suggested figurative comparison of stones to sons, what words from these first two verses of Lamentations reinforce and develop the writer's theme?

---

10. Assigning a number of sentences to a paragraph is just a suggestion. An excellent paragraph may explain its topic in two or three sentences. A paragraph of seven sentences might benefit from some editing to make sure each sentence pertains to the paragraph's topic, or it might be that each sentence is essential to the paragraph's development. Even expository writing is an art, so it resists rigid rules.

CONTEXT—A FACTOR IN HERMENEUTICS

Jeremiah grieves over the state of the "precious sons of Zion." *Precious* is a word that demands a closer look. Its etymological origins include words such as *price, value,* and even *honor.*[11] But these etymological roots do not explain *why* something is costly or valuable, or *who* values or honors it. Is there something inherent in the person or item called "precious" that gives it its value and requires it to be honored? Contextually contrasting quotations from Revelation show that *why, who,* and *how* questions lead us to consider contextual details that can strengthen our hermeneutical reliability.

Most of the references to precious stones in Scripture are references to literal gems that may also have symbolic significance because of their kind and number.[12] In the Apostle John's description of the New Jerusalem, many of the same stones previously mentioned in Scripture adorn the foundation of the City of God:

> The foundations of the city walls were decorated with every kind of precious stone. The first foundation was jasper, the second sapphire, the third chalcedony, the fourth emerald, the fifth sardonyx, the sixth carnelian, the seventh chrysolite, the eighth beryl, the ninth topaz, the tenth chrysoprase, the eleventh jacinth, and the twelfth amethyst.[13]

Leaving aside many interesting questions about the kinds and number of stones mentioned here and their individual implicit and explicit symbolic meanings, we will focus on the adjective describing them as "precious."

We think of precious stones in terms of some characteristic quality tied to their value—they are rare, difficult to mine, brilliantly colored, and so on. But when we look at how they are being used, we are looking at context. The stones of this Revelation

11. Cresswell, *Oxford Dictionary,* 342–343.

12. Exodus 28, for instance, specifies that the twelve stones of Aaron's breastplate represent the twelve tribes of Israel.

13. Rev 21:19–20 NIV.

passage are precious because of the kinds of stones they are (rare and beautiful), but also because of the way they are being used (to decorate the City of God).

We find a very different context for the adjective *precious* in an earlier passage in John's Revelation. Chapter 17 describes a symbol of great evil and monstrous hatred for Christ and his people. A foil[14] for the City of God, the figurative city of Babylon is symbolized as a woman who

> was dressed in purple and scarlet, and was glittering with gold, precious stones and pearls. She held a golden cup in her hand, filled with abominable things and . . . filth.[15]

All of the beautiful elements of this woman's adornment are used elsewhere in Scripture to opposite ends. The colors of her sumptuous attire are those prescribed by God for the construction of a sanctuary wherein he "may dwell in [his people's] midst."[16] A pearl of exceptional value is the basis of Jesus's parabolic comparison to the kingdom of God.[17] The City of God and its measuring rod are gold, juxtaposed here with the woman's "golden cup." The stones decorating this symbol of heinousness are deemed "precious" as are the stones adorning the foundation of the City of God.

The contextual clues signifying a different interpretation for the beautiful items in this chapter are not subtle. John's unequivocal diction describes the golden cup's contents ("filled with abominable things") and the nature of the one who is decorated ("mother of prostitutes and of earth's abominations.")[18] Because the gold, beautiful colors, precious stones and pearls are being used in this context to decorate an enemy of God and his people, they are offensive and worthless baubles. Their beautiful qualities

---

14. A literary foil is a character (usually) who stands in contrast to another character to emphasize the differences between both.

15. Rev 17:4 NIV.

16. Ex 25:3, 4, 8.

17. Matt 13:45–46.

18. Rev 17:5.

are specious.[19] Any apparent beauty in this cloth, jewel, and cup is judged as hideously ugly because of the way this symbolic woman behaves toward Christ and his Church: she is "drunk with the blood of the saints, the blood of the martyrs of Jesus."[20] This contextualized reading of *precious* answers our question about whether there is anything inherent in a person or item—apart from God—that deems it valuable or honorable. It also reminds us that what is precious according to the world's standards may not be precious in the sight of God and vice versa[21].

Some people may think that John is misogynistic[22] in choosing to symbolize this unspeakably evil power as a woman. Our modern sensibilities are also troubled by accusations of prostitution and adultery that seem to be leveled solely at the woman, ignoring her consorts. It's important to recognize that our modern sensibilities are themselves a contextual framework affecting our intellectual and moral reactions. These modern sensibilities must be measured against Biblical usage and context rightly understood. Prostitution and adultery are indeed affronts to the holy God; yet their mention is sometimes contextualized within the Biblical doctrine of grace that runs throughout the Old and New Testaments. We think of Rahab the prostitute who is included in Christ's own genealogy[23] and mentioned alongside Abraham by the Lord's brother James as an example of faith.[24] We recall Jesus's words to the adulterous woman who was to be stoned according to Mosaic Law,[25] and his conversation with the Samaritan woman at the well.[26] We must also take the allegorical story of Hosea and

19. *specious* (*spee*-schus) means misleadingly attractive.

20. Rev 17:6.

21. See Ps 72:12–14 and 1 Pet 2:4.

22. *misogynistic* (mih-saw-jan-*is*-tic) displaying strongly negative attitudes toward women. Etymology: miso (hate) + gune (woman). Hoad, *Concise Oxford*, 296.

23. Matt 1:5.

24. Jas 2:21–25.

25. John 8:3–11.

26. John 4:7–42.

his adulterous wife Gomer into account. And, we must read John's description of the great prostitute of chapter 17 alongside John's earlier use of a woman as a symbol.[27] In this earlier context, the woman symbolizes God's chosen people and their struggle against Satan. This is the opposite of the meaning of the Rev. 17 passage. It's probably not hyperbolic to insist that context is everything; text without context *is* pretext.

Context helps us understand rightly—or at least avoid unnecessarily serious error. This is true whether we are reading the Bible or anything else, including people. (Yes, we read people, and when we misread them it is often because we have overlooked contextual information.) Sometimes stones are precious ornaments. Sometimes they are stumbling blocks.[28] Sometimes they are weapons (e.g. David's "five smooth stones"[29]) or pillows.[30] Sometimes they mark boundaries between people's property lines. Sometimes they serve as foundations. We need to know the surrounding context (in the chapter and in the whole of Scripture[31]) in order to justly interpret the text.

Written Response #2: Read through the Biblical passages that follow; then, write a persuasive essay of four or five paragraphs on one of the following propositions: [32]

1. God contradicts himself in telling the Jews to erect a stone monument in Joshua 4 yet punishing the Jews for erecting monuments in other instances.

---

27. Rev 12:1–6, 13–17.

28. Sometimes these stumbling blocks are linked to the Gospel; sometimes they are linked to Satan.

29. 1 Sam 17:40.

30. Jacob's pillow in Gen. 28:11.

31. The Westminster Confession identifies an important hermeneutic principle in 1:9 that is often summarized by the dictum "Scripture interprets Scripture."

32. A term of debate, a proposition states a theory or opinion that is then debated.

2. God is partial to his chosen people, the Jews. He punishes Gentiles for behaviors that he overlooks in the Israelites.

State the controversy and your position in the opening paragraph. Include fragments of three different quotations in the body paragraphs.[33] Cite your quotations using parenthetical citations or footnotes, as I've done in this book. Write a brief, clear, concluding paragraph, but do not merely restate your introduction (see example of a persuasive essay in chapter 9).

The following quotations are the figurative stones on which you will build your persuasive essay. Each of these selected passages says something about "sacred stones." Suggestions for building your essay ("Preparation") are found at the end of the quote selections.

Quotation #1:
This is what you are to do to them: Break down their altars, smash their sacred stones, cut down their Asherah poles and burn their idols in the fire.[34]

Quotation #2:
Break down their altars, smash their sacred stones and burn their Asherah poles in the fire; cut down the idols of their gods and wipe out their names from those places.[35]

Quotation #3:
And do not erect a sacred stone, for these the LORD your God hates.[36]

---

33. See ch. 6 for more on fragment (run in) quotations. I've used them frequently throughout this book.

34. Deut 7:5 NIV.

35. Deut 12:3 NIV.

36. Deut 16:22 NIV.

Quotation #4:
They brought the sacred stone out of the temple of Baal and burned it. They demolished the sacred stone of Baal and tore down the temple of Baal, and people have used it for a latrine to this day.[37]

Quotation #5:
He removed the high places, smashed the sacred stones and cut down the Asherah poles. He broke into pieces the bronze snake Moses had made, for up to that time the Israelites had been burning incense to it. (It was called Nehushtan.) [38]

Quotation #6:
For the Israelites will live many days without king or prince, without sacrifice or sacred stones, without ephod or idol.[39]

Quotation #7:
Israel was a spreading vine; he brought forth fruit for himself. As his fruit increased, he built more altars; as his land prospered, he adorned his sacred stones. [40]

Quotation #8:
I will destroy your carved images and your sacred stones from among you; you will no longer bow down to the work of your hands.[41]

Preparation:

1. Read through each quotation to determine the group of people for whom the stones are sacred. Why are the stones considered sacred? If you need further context, look up the quotation (the phrase "sacred stones" used in the NIV is translated as "pillars" in the ESV).

---

37. 2 Kgs 10:26-27 NIV.
38. 2 Kgs 18:4 NIV.
39. Hos 3:4 NIV.
40. Hos 10:1 NIV.
41. Mic 5:13 NIV.

2. Underline or highlight key words. Key words include words that are repeated, or words that are strongly emotional in tone.[42]

3. Ask questions: Whose emotions are described in these tone words? Is there more than one tone? Is there more than one person or group in the quotation?

4. What quotations seem most similar in their entirety? Where do these similar quotations differ? Do differences shed contextual light on other similar quotations?

---

42. *Tone* refers to the emotional impact of diction. Consider the speaker's tone toward himself, his topic, and/or his audience. Nouns identify tone. Examples include *calm* or *peacefulness, sympathy, tenderness, joy, sorrow, grief, bitterness, anger* or *rage, violence, shame, sarcasm,* etc. Adjectives, adverbs, and participles describe tone: (*joyfully, pleading, angered, sarcastic,* etc.).

4

What Do These Stones Mean?

PARENTS WERE CHARGED WITH conveying a powerful narrative to their children when they asked this question. Joshua's instruction for the narrative's content is clear: "'Let your children know'" that

> 'Israel passed over this Jordan on dry ground.' For the LORD your God dried up the waters of the Jordan for you until you passed over, as the LORD your God did to the Red Sea, which he dried up for us until we passed over, so that all the peoples of the earth may know that the hand of the LORD is mighty, that you may fear the LORD your God forever.[1]

In this brief direction, just two sentences in the ESV translation, Joshua explains the significance of this stone memorial and its accompanying narrative for the children of Israel and for all the peoples of the earth. We might wonder whether all questions about meaning may not be best answered in this direct and literal manner.

The question about how meaning is communicated lies at the heart of all human experience. When Jesus tells his disciples, "I have said these things to you in figures of speech. The hour is

---

1. Josh 4:22–24

coming when I will no longer speak to you in figures of speech but will tell you plainly about the Father," his disciples' relief is unmistakable: "Ah, now you are speaking plainly and not using figurative speech!"[2] Yet the extensive presence of figurative language throughout Scripture is a strong argument for its necessity and efficacy in communicating the things of God to humankind.

The obvious question is *why?* Why is direct, factual language not always the preferred method of truthful discourse? It is a question too multifaceted for this author to understand or answer, but let me take one facet and extend it for your own consideration. You might consider how and why the symbols of scientific and mathematic languages differ from the symbols of words in communicating truth. You might consider the language of music and the differences and unities between its sound and its notation. You might consider choreology and the dance. You might consider an artist's canvas and ask yourself what part the medium of paint plays in conveying meaning. You might consider what part the negative space used by the painter, sculptor, photographer and poet, or the silence used by the playwright or the composer of music contributes to the "whole picture." These many languages, though different, have this in common: the gap existing between the sign and the meaning or reality it signifies.[3] No human expression can adequately bridge this gap. In the Incarnation, however, the Logos did just that.

JESUS'S DISCOURSE

Among our favorite quotations of our Lord's words are probably some in which he uses metaphors or other figurative language, but Jesus did not always speak figuratively. In the week preceding his crucifixion, for instance, after some were commenting on the splendor of the (second) temple and, "how it was adorned with noble stones and offerings, [Jesus says], 'As for these things that

2. John 16:25, 29

3. See The Westminster Confession of Faith (27.2) on the sacraments as a sign.

you see, the days will come when there will not be left here one stone upon another that will not be thrown down."[4] Jesus is speaking literally, prophesying the actual destruction of this amazingly beautiful and massively large-stoned temple. His prophecy was fulfilled around 70 AD[5] when the temple was destroyed.[6]

Jesus also speaks of the temple figuratively. When the unbelieving Jews demand a sign from him that would verify his authority, Jesus replies using the temple as a metaphor for his body, saying,

> "Destroy this temple, and in three days I will raise it up."

The Jews did not understand that he was speaking figuratively, so they said,

> "It has taken forty-six years to build this temple, and will
> you raise it up in three days?" But he was speaking about
> the temple of his body.[7]

At one point, Jesus explains that he speaks in parables so that the Pharisees would not understand "the secrets of the kingdom of heaven."[8] Sometimes, however, the Pharisees do understand the import of Jesus's figures of speech, and they correctly deduce that he is criticizing them. After telling the parable of the wicked tenants, Jesus asks them,

---

4. Luke 21:5–6. Punctuate a quotation within a quotation by using single quotation marks for the inner quote.

5. AD (Anno Domini) is a Latin abbreviation for "the year of the Lord." It is more frequently referred to as CE (common era) in contemporary works. Similarly, BC ("before Christ") has been replaced in many publications with BCE ("before common era"). The change in language is initiated by cultural usage and reflects the shifts in culture.

6. Astute readers who researched the Western or Wailing Wall alluded to in ch.1 of this book are encouraged to research this question. https://www.christiancourier.com/articles/1302-jesus-prophecy-and-the-destruction-of-the-temple offers one explanation.

7. John 2:18–21 NIV. Block (indented) quotations omit quotation marks, except when dialogue is a part of the indented quotation, as it is in this example.

8. Matt 13:11, 13.

"Have you not read this Scripture: 'the stone that the builders rejected / has become the cornerstone; / this was the Lord's doing, / and it is marvelous in our eyes'"? [9]

The chief priests, scribes and elders "were seeking to arrest him but feared the people, for they perceived that he had told the parable against them."[10]

Written Response #3: Jesus's office as Prophet (he is Prophet, Priest, and King) is verified in both his literal and figurative statements about "the temple." This assignment focuses on Jesus's office as Prophet. You may also write about these passages[11] as evidence of his office as Priest and his office as King if you wish.

1. Write two sentences explaining the way in which each of these prophecies was fulfilled—one sentence explaining the fulfillment of the literal prophecy about the temple's future destruction and one sentence explaining the fulfillment of the figurative prophecy about the temple of his body.

2. Read the accounts of specific insults hurled at Jesus as he suffered on the cross (Matt. 27:39–42 and Mark 15:29–31). Are the mockers speaking of a literal or figurative temple?

3. Explain the irony of these mockers' insults.[12] Which of the three kinds of irony briefly defined in the footnote below best identifies this particular irony?

Written Response #4: (Exposition) Write a brief explanation (200–300 words) of the truth taught through the use of figurative language in the quotations below.

Preparation:

9. Mark 12:10–11. (Jesus is quoting Ps. 118:22.)

10. Mark 12:12.

11. John 2:19-21, Luke 21:5-6, Mark 13:1-2, and Matt. 24: 1-2

12. *Irony:* a contrast between 1) what a person says and what (s)he actually means (*verbal irony*), 2) what is expected and what happens instead (*situational irony*), or 3) what the speaker means and what the hearers or readers understand from the speaker's words (*dramatic irony*).

1. Look up each of the verses. Read some of the verses or chapters before and after the quotation in order to get a sense of the context in which Jesus, Paul, or Peter is speaking. Context will help you identify the "who" of personal pronouns such as *them, you, our,* and *us.*

2. *Tip:* You'll want to begin by making sure you understand the specific quality or qualities of the stone in each quotation. List them.

3. You may also want to write the questions you have to see if you can find answers to these questions before you begin your writing. For instance, why would builders, who use stones to build, reject a stone? And, what, exactly is a cornerstone? What function does a cornerstone serve in constructing a building? Maybe you have other questions. *Questions are keys to understanding. Don't ignore them!* In fact, the more questions you encounter as you plan and write, the more interesting your essay will likely be. It will probably be more insightful or convincing than the quick pat answers often offered.

4. Feel free to look up definitions for words (e.g., *cornerstone*), but resist the temptation to consult commentaries or other sources that offer interpretations of the assigned quotations. The purpose of these writing responses is the development of strong hermeneutical thinking. While it is true that consulting a source of someone else's thinking can sometimes serve as a model of how to think, it can also be a substitute for thinking. There may also be more than one good way to think about the question.

Quotation #1:
Jesus said to them, "Have you never read in the Scriptures: 'The stone that the builders rejected / has become the cornerstone; / this was the Lord's doing, / and it is marvelous in our eyes'"?[13]

---

13. Matt 21:42.

Quotation #2:

And you show that you are a letter from Christ delivered by us, written not with ink but with the Spirit of the living God, not on tablets of stone but on tablets of human hearts.[14]

Quotation #3:

As you come to him, a living stone rejected by men but in the sight of God chosen and precious, you yourselves like living stones are being built up as a spiritual house.[15]

Quotation #4:

I tell you, God is able from these stones to raise up children for Abraham.[16]

Quotation #5:

And he will become a sanctuary and a stone of offense and a rock of stumbling to both houses of Israel, a trap and a snare to the inhabitants of Jerusalem.[17]

Think about this: In our various translations of Scripture, Satan, the "father of lies," does not use figurative language in his deceptions. He questions Eve's understanding of God's command, he informs God that he roams the earth, and he challenges Jesus to "tell these stones to become bread"; but these are not examples of figurative language. His "skin for skin"[18] comment to God is generally recognized as a proverb, not a figure of speech. When Jesus tells Peter that Satan has asked to "sift you like wheat,"[19] it is Jesus restating Satan's demand.

14. 2 Cor 3:3.
15. 1 Pet 2:4–5a.
16. Matt 3.9b and Luke 3.8b.
17. Isa 8:14. See also 1 Pe 2:6–8.
18. Job 2.4.
19. Luke 22:31b.

5

A Visual Approach
Drawing Symbolic Images[1]

SOME DRAWINGS, PAINTINGS, AND sculptures are admired for their realistic representation. They look remarkably similar to the humans, animals, or bowls of fruit they represent. Not all representational art has symbolic meaning, but some does. For instance, a realistically drawn bowl of rotting fruit vividly pictures the reality of decay and death.

Nonrepresentational art eschews representation (hence the name!). Its colors, shapes, lines, and media encourage a different kind of viewing experience. Using the language of literary terms, we might describe this viewing experience as one that prefers and exploits connotative associations over denotative definitions.

Sculptures and monuments fashioned to symbolically memorialize an event or person differ widely. Some, such as Mount

1. Think about the difference between drawing or sculpting images and the prohibition of the Second Commandment. What does the Commandment prohibit? Consider also whether there is any difference between drawing an image and downloading an image from the Internet that someone else has made in terms of the Commandment's intention (i.e., is there a difference between whether you or someone else makes or draws an image that you're using for some purpose?)

Rushmore, the Statue of Liberty, and several Holocaust memorials, depict their subjects representationally. Appreciation of these memorials is enhanced by historical context, but the viewer probably infers[2] something about their meaning even without explanatory input. Lady Liberty raises a lamp, and her feet are encircled by broken shackles. Most viewers perceive the joy of freedom she depicts. Historical context helps us further understand that the statue implies freedom from ideological and physical slavery.

The twelve stones of Gilgal are not intended as art in the usual sense of the word—a word that is notoriously difficult to define. They provide a memorial, the meaning of which is not visually representational. Neither are they nonrepresentational, since their very substance as stones taken from and situated alongside the Jordan River over which the Israelites crossed speaks to their symbolic significance. They link image and story in a way that harmonizes the two impulses. Yet, while Lady Liberty's historical meaning depends upon narrative for greater contextualization, the meaning of the Gilgal stones is entirely dependent upon the narrative.

This dependency upon narrative may have been the design of the Architect God. The stones are amassed in some form, but the details of their arrangement are not included in Joshua's record. The memorial's purpose for Israel is to connect generations with their covenantal God, and this is aided by the telling and retelling of the essential story. Children would look at the stones and ask questions. Parents or grandparents would explain that the stones are a reminder of God's power over nature and his faithfulness to and provision for his people.

This chapter asks you to imagine and draw images symbolizing power and provision. Your drawings may fall anywhere along the representational—nonrepresentational spectrum. They may pertain to God's power and provision or to the power and provision he grants or permits to human individuals and systems.[3]

2. *Infer* means to deduce or to conclude. Do not confuse it with *imply*, which means to suggest something indirectly. (See note 5, ch. 1)

3. See John 19:10–11, Ps 20:6–7, and Jer 9:23–24 for instance.

TRY IT! #3

1. On the following pages, or on separate paper, draw at least two images symbolizing power and at least two images symbolizing provision:

Two images	→	symbolizing	→	Power
Two images	→	symbolizing	→	Provision

2. On the lines provided, follow your drawings with a critique exploring the similarities and differences between your drawings. Consider some of the following questions when drawing your images and when critiquing them:

Power: What is the source of this power (electrical, political, etc.)? Who or what possesses or controls the power imaged in your drawing? Can anyone possess this power, or does it belong to a certain individual or group? How is this power exercised and for what purpose? What might happen if this power were lost to the individual (or group) who possesses it?

Provision: What is provided (food, shelter, friendship, etc.), by whom, and for whom? What is the relationship between the provider and the provided for? Why is this provision needed? How is this provision delivered? What might happen if this provision were not available? Is anyone excluded from receiving this provision?

- Images   →   symbolizing   →   Power

- These images symbolizing power are similar because _____

  _____

  _____

  _____

  _____

- These images symbolizing power are different because (e.g. power is portrayed as comforting or inspiring in one image but threatening in another, etc.) [4] _____

  _____

  _____

  _____

  _____

4. Recall that birds, a common symbol, symbolize different and sometimes contradictory ideas. See ch. 2.

- Images   →   symbolizing   →   Provision

- These images symbolizing provision are similar because ___
  _____
  _____
  _____
  _____
  _____

- These images symbolizing provision are different because
  (e.g. provision is necessary in one image and superfluous in
  the other, etc.) _____
  _____
  _____
  _____
  _____

Written Response #5: Persuasive mode.

What caveat is implied about images as symbols of abstractions?[5] Does a light bulb always and only symbolize an idea, or might it suggest a different concept? Do you think that someone from another culture or time period might have a different interpretation of the light bulb?

Apply these questions (or any others that these generate) to your own drawings and to the answers you have written beneath your drawings. You may write your answer as a bullet point or as a finished paragraph of at least three to five sentences. Whether you write a paragraph or a set of bullet points, be specific in your persuasive argument about the benefits and detriments of using drawn symbols to convey ideas. If you use the following bullet points, your sentence completions should be thoughtful and insightful. Don't even think about completing the first bullet point, for instance, with the elementary observation that "they create a picture in our minds."

- Images that depict abstractions are helpful because . . .

- Images that depict abstractions may sometimes be unhelpful or confusing because . . .

Your response should take a position, but if you are undecided, simply list the two or more sides of the argument. You are encouraged to illustrate your points with drawings!

STORYBOARDING

Storyboarding (putting written stories into graphic form) is a useful means of visualization and organization. Writers of all kinds (novelists, advertisers, dramatists, screenwriters, video game creators, etc.) use storyboards in their writing process. The storyboard

---

5. Rene Magritte dealt with one aspect of this problem in his painting entitled "The Treachery of Images." The question asked above is related to this chapter and also to chapter 4. It is useful to discussions of the Second Commandment as well as to philosophical inquiries into the nature of being.

may even substitute for text as the primary medium of the story, as in graphic novels.

TRY IT! #4

Several templates for storyboarding are available online. Text is still important, but the emphasis is upon the visual.

Create a storyboard for the description Daniel offers of King Nebuchadnezzar's dream vision from the book of Daniel. Read the surrounding passages to check and inform your understanding of the selected verses; then, plan and draw your storyboard.

> As you looked, a stone was cut out by no human hand, and it struck the image on its feet of iron and clay, and broke them in pieces. Then the iron, the clay, the bronze, the silver, and the gold, all together were broken in pieces, and became like the chaff of the summer threshing floors; and the wind carried them away, so that not a trace of them could be found. But the stone that struck the image became a great mountain and filled the whole earth.[6]

6. Dan 2.34–35.

6

Quotations as Building Stones

How to Fit These Supporting Elements into Your Expository and Persuasive Writing

ACADEMIC WRITING IN PERSUASIVE and expository modes requires references to other sources. Whether you summarize, paraphrase, or directly quote the other sources, you must provide a citation. Any information or idea that you take from another source to put into your own writing must be cited unless it is considered "common knowledge." Several reliable sites explaining what constitutes common knowledge may be found online. I've cited one below.[1]

When a writing assignment requires you to consult sources, invest time in locating, reading, and taking notes from those that seem promising. Don't rush through this part; it greatly affects the quality of your finished project. (These are the stones, the foundation of your finished structure.) Summarize and paraphrase most of your relevant source material, but include *some* (about 10–20% of your paper) well-chosen quoted material to lend support and build interest.

1. https://integrity.mit.edu/handbook/citing-your-sources/what-common-knowledge

Depending upon the length of your selected quotations, you will either indent them in a block, or you will work a fragment of the quotation into your own sentence, a technique also referred to as a run in quotation. Examples of each form of direct quotation may be found throughout *Stones and Stories,* but this chapter provides a fuller explanation.

Assume you've been assigned an essay explaining the "sacred stone" referred to by the town clerk in this passage from the book of Acts of the Apostles:

> And when the town clerk had quieted the crowd, he said, "Men of Ephesus, who is there who does not know that the city of the Ephesians is temple keeper of the great Artemis, and of the sacred stone that fell from the sky? Seeing then that these things cannot be denied, you ought to be quiet and do nothing rash."[2]

The passage offers many research possibilities: pagan reactions to the spread of the early Christian church, the connection between the Greek goddess Artemis and the Roman goddess Diana, the economic and gender underpinnings of the Ephesian riot, and the authority granted a town clerk in first century Greece among them. Your assignment, however, narrows the field: you're to focus on the sacred stone. Many excellent papers have received disappointing grades because they answered a question that was not asked in the assignment.

You've researched a number of sources. You've visited a library or at least risen above an initial Google search. You've eliminated sources that are off-topic no matter how interesting they are. You've checked the academic credibility of your sources. You've written electronic or paper notes (including but not limited to those you have cut and pasted), and you've selected your key quotations. One of these direct quotations offers the following information:

> Certain small stones, called in Greek *baituloi* and *baitulia,* which were often, if not always, meteorites and held

---

2. Acts 19:35–36.

sacred because they fell from heaven, played a part in gentile superstition. They were said to move, talk, and guard from evil. The Greek name, if it had a Semitic origin, as there is scarcely reason to doubt, is akin to *beth'el* and may indicate that the stone was regarded as the abode of a supernatural power, spirit, or god. The name was not used by the Semites to designate the rude stone pillars which they set up at places of worship (Deut. xii. 3; see HIGH PLACES).[3]

You need to decide whether this quotation should be included in its entirety, or whether fragmented portions would be more effective. As you write your report, you want to use quotations of different lengths, with more run in than block quotations. Style manuals differ on the number of words that necessitate a blocked quotation. Choose one style guide or follow the instructions you've been given, and be consistent. If the passage you wish to quote is shorter than, say, forty words, it is best to work the quotation into your own writing by using a run in technique. There may be legitimate reasons to break this rule. Perhaps your brief quotation requires the attention that a block quotation affords. Most style manuals address these exceptions.

BLOCK (INDENTED) QUOTATIONS

- The quotation above appears exactly as it does in *Davis Dictionary of the Bible*; therefore, it is termed a direct quotation. Because it is a lengthy (100 words) quotation, it is indented, and the quotation marks are omitted. Quotation marks are unnecessary because its indentation identifies it as a quotation. When your blocked quotation includes dialogue, however, as the Acts 19 passage does, use double quotation marks around the dialogue.

- The quotation is cited with a footnote. Other styles of documentation, such as those used by MLA, place the citation in

---

3. Davis, *Davis Dictionary of the Bible*, 787.

parentheses immediately following the quotation as *Davis Dictionary* has done with the Deuteronomy reference.

FRAGMENT (RUN IN) QUOTATIONS

- The block quotations above have not been altered in any way. They have not eliminated or changed any word or punctuation. It is sometimes preferable, however, to select just that portion of the quoted material that suits your purpose— eliminating words, changing tense, and making any other alterations necessary for grammaticality and graceful flow.

- The skillful manipulator[4] respects the quoted material and the rules concerning the handling of quotations. It is absolutely essential that you copy quotations correctly, using brackets and ellipses to indicate any alterations or omissions you have made to the original material (even a piece of punctuation or a changed tense). Brackets are often necessary for the sake of tense consistency, but there are other occasions requiring this signal that the original quotation has been altered or manipulated. An ellipsis[5] is used to indicate omitted words, phrases, or sentences. The following fragment quotations have been manipulated for tense consistency and grammaticality. Brackets and an ellipsis indicate the changed portions:

    a. *Some Greeks believed that these small stones "move[d], talk[ed], and guard[ed] from evil."*[6]

---

4. *Manipulator* is a loaded word, meaning that it has different denotations and connotations. As the next section explains, it is used here to mean skillful handling without malicious intent. In fact, the skillful handling seeks to facilitate right understanding.

5. An ellipsis consists of three dots or periods (four if omission includes a sentence end and picks up with new sentence) indicating that the original quotation has been cut. Plural = ellipses.

6. Davis, *Davis Dictionary of the Bible*, 787.

b. *The dictionary editors, noting similarities between the Greek word for small stone and the Hebrew word,* beth'el, *which means house of God, infer that such "stone[s] w[ere] regarded as the abode of a supernatural power, spirit, or god."*[7]

c. *The reason that "certain small stones . . . [were] held sacred" among some Greeks is simply "because they fell from heaven."*[8]

MANIPULATING QUOTED MATERIAL

This point bears repeating: The word *manipulate* has different connotations and denotations. Its two very different denotations are "to handle material with skill," and "to handle material with intent to deceive or mislead." Someone will point out here that a convincing deception requires skill, and that the two denotations are therefore related. It's an interesting argument, so let me put the definitions in an ethical context: *When necessary, the ethical writer manipulates quoted material in a skillful manner, making sure that his or her manipulation does not cross over into an unethical area of deception or propaganda.*

In choosing your supporting quotations, you must not take a quotation out of a context that is essential to the quotation's meaning. You must not eliminate those portions of the quotation that contradict your point. If you do, you are manipulating the quoted material in an unethical way. Chapter 3 discussed the great importance of context. It is possible—and dishonest—to manipulate a quotation by ignoring its context so as to distort its meaning. For instance, if you manipulate the *Davis Dictionary* quotation in the following manner:

> The similarity between the Greek word for these stones, *baituloi,* and the Hebrew word *beth'el* suggests that the

7. Davis, *Davis Dictionary of the Bible,* 787.

8. Davis, *Davis Dictionary of the Bible,* 787. Note the spacing of the ellipsis. Do not eliminate spaces between each dot or period.

> Israelites believed that these stones were "the abode of a
> supernatural power, spirit, or god" [9]

you would have used quoted material within a paraphrase that
distorts the meaning of the source you have quoted. Even though
you have cited your source as you must, your distortion would be
a form of lying, as it would deceive your reader/audience and bear
false witness against the quoted author, whose words mean something very different. (So if the tone and diction of this paragraph's
beginning sound like that of the Ten Commandments, it's because
of the prohibition of the ninth Commandment.)

Written or Oral Response: Debate the following proposition.
Proposition: Manipulating quoted material is similar in purpose
to using figurative language.

---

9. Davis, *Davis Dictionary of the Bible*, 787.

7

Writing a Research Report

FOR THE PURPOSE OF this chapter, we will distinguish between a research paper and a research report by defining a *research paper* as a paper that proposes and argues an idea, and a *research report* as a paper that transmits information. This chapter offers writing modes best suited for producing *research reports.*

Look through the writing topic suggestions that follow. After you've chosen a topic that interests you, spend time (as instructed in chapter 6) locating, reading, and taking notes from reliable sources. Note-taking is preferable to cutting and pasting because it forces you to understand your material and guards you against unintentional plagiarism. Much of your report will summarize or paraphrase your sources, but about 10–20 percent of your report should be quoted material. Dictionaries and Wikipedia are sometimes helpful beginning places; they can provide basic vocabulary and context for your topic and suggest further sources to research. They are not your end in research, however, and you should not consider Wikipedia a source for summary, paraphrase, or quotation. Look for some print sources; these are validated as academically respectable, whereas not all electronic sources can claim similar reliability. An important intellectual tool in research is the ability to determine the reliability of any source. Topic #13 below lists some preliminary criteria for evaluating sources. Online sites offer additional direction.

Written Response #6: Review the list of topics and the five instructions that follow; then, write a report of your research.

1. Number of sources: 3 or more. Length of report: 1,000–1,750 words (including citations). The length of your report depends upon your topic choice; some topics have more available material to research. Topics with an abundance of material require you to narrow your research compilation, an important skill.

2. Summarize or paraphrase the key points of each source. A summary is shorter than a paraphrase. It condenses the original into main points. A paraphrase is broader in scope than a summary, but it is still shorter than the original passage. Whether summarizing or paraphrasing, you must use your own words rather than the source author's words. This requires more than changing a few words in the original. If your paraphrase is too close to the original, you may be guilty of plagiarism, even though you cite your paraphrase.

3. Select key quotations (quoted material key to the report topic that cannot be just as effectively summarized or paraphrased). Whether you decide to fragment or indent your quotations, you should choose carefully, eliminating that which is easily summarized and quoting only the gem portion(s).

4. Cite summaries, paraphrases, and quotations (you may choose to use footnotes, endnotes, or parenthetical documentation,[1] but be consistent). Review your notes and reorganize your material so that each paragraph does not merely paraphrase one source. Aim for at least two different sources in each paragraph to avoid the unimpressive single footnote at the end of each paragraph.

---

1. APA and CMOS use footnotes or endnotes; MLA uses parentheses in the body of the research paper. A good reference site is Purdue OWL (Online Writing Lab) at https://owl.english.purdue.edu/owl/

5. You won't use the persuasive mode of writing since it is more appropriate for a research paper that offers the researcher's thesis or opinion about the research topic. You may incorporate the narrative mode, however. For instance, if you choose topic #18 because your aunt and uncle are geologists, you could personalize (but don't pad) your report with a story about their experiences.

RESEARCH REPORT TOPICS

Stones are found everywhere—in the physical world and in art, literature, and commerce. We cannot learn all there is to know about literal and figurative stones, but the more we think about them, the more we appreciate the vastness of this topic. You just need a place to start. So here are some suggestions.

1. *Report* on the definition and etymology of these compound stone words: cobblestone, brimstone, millstone, touchstone, keystone, stonewall, and/or cornerstone.

2. *Explain* the physics of skipping stones across water.

3. *Describe* some of the world's notable stone structures: Easter Island Statues (Chile), Sacsayhuaman (Peru), Teotihuacan (Mexico), Yonaguni (Japan), Imba Huru (Zimbabwe), Ziggurat of Ur (Iraq), Obelisk of Axum (Ethiopia), Devil's Arrows (England) Newgrange (Ireland) Sueno's Stone (Scotland) Calanais Stones (Scotland) Pictish stones (various sites) Stonehenge (England) Chaco Canyon (New Mexico), Cliff Dwellers Mesa Verde Stone circles (Colorado, USA).

4. *Describe* some of the world's famous stone bridges: Puente Nuevo (Spain), Bastei Bridge, (Saxon Switzerland Park Germany), Rialto Bridge (Italy), Ponte Vecchio (Italy), Khaju Bridge (Iran), Charles Bridge (Czech Rep.), Pont Neuf (Paris), Stari Most (Bosnia & Herzegovina), Puente de Piedra (Spain), Konitsa (Greece). See "Stone bridge" in Wikipedia for additional examples.

5. *Explain* the figurative and/or literal uses of stones in Shakespeare's sonnets. Stones are mentioned in four sonnets, #52, #55, #65, and #94. You can find these four sonnets at https://www.opensourceshakespeare.org/concordance/. You may consult Shakespeare scholars for this report. If you write a paper arguing for one interpretation over another (instead of merely reporting your findings), use the persuasive mode. If you write a paper proposing your own interpretation, use the expository mode.

6. *Review* the differences among basic stone or rock formations such as sedimentary, metamorphic, and igneous.

7. *List* and *describe* the artistic use of stones in projects such as inlay, mosaic, mandala, and cairns.

8. *Report* on stones used as currency, e.g. Rai stones.

9. *Explain* the use of stones in music e.g., lithophone and sounding stone.

10. *Outline* and *explain* common phrases and proverbs about stones. Abundant examples include a rolling stone gathers no moss, stepping stone, a stone's throw, kill two birds with one stone, to carve (or set) in stone, you can't get blood from a stone, leave no stone unturned.

11. Research some of the following famous stones, then *explain* the basis of their fame by constructing an *outline*: the Sorcerer's Stone, Garuda Stone, Rosetta Stone, London Stone, the sword in the stone, the Blarney Stone, Sisyphus's Stone, Stone Soup, Atlas turned to stone, Medusa's gaze which turned people to stone, the Foundation Stone.

12. Research and *report* on three or more commentaries dealing with the devil's first temptation to Christ: "If you are the Son of God, command these stones to become loaves of bread." Look for differences in commentators' information and/or interpretation.

13. Research the Jewish practice of placing stones atop grave markers (the movie *Schindler's List* ends with this image). You will find some differences in explanatory information in

at least three different online sources. Your research report should *summarize* the material and include one *quotation* from each source that differs in content from the other two (or more) sources. Offer your opinion about the sources' reliability based upon each site's name and domain, the authors' credentials, and the way the information is presented (word choice, paragraph or bullets, use of images, font choice and size, hyperlinks, spelling, grammatical precision, bibliography, etc.). This source annotation may be included in the body of your research report or added in an appendix.

14. *Recount* your findings on the way(s) stones are formed. You may wish to include answers to the following questions: What criteria differentiate stones from rocks or pebbles? How much of the earth is made of stone? What about space stones such as meteorites or asteroids?

15. Read about and *report* on the architectural use of stones and at least one other material, synthetic or natural. How many of our buildings are made of stone? Is natural stone used in new construction? How stable are stone buildings?

16. *Explain* why some stones used in jewelry are more expensive than others.

17. *Document* the involvement of stones (e.g. "blood diamonds," child labor in mining industry) in human misery.

18. *List* a variety of occupations available to people who are interested in stones (e.g., geologists, gemologists, artists, architects). What kind of training is necessary? What does the job require a person to do?

19. *Compare* and/or *contrast* three or more commentaries on the mysterious Urim and the Thummim mentioned in Exod. 28:30 and elsewhere (use a Bible concordance to locate additional references).

20. *Compare* and/or *contrast* three or more commentaries on the mysterious white stone mentioned in Rev. 2:17.

8

Creative Writing

POEMS

I have always thought of poems as stepping stones in one's own sense of oneself. Every now and again, you write a poem that gives you self-respect and steadies your going a little bit farther out in the stream. At the same time, you have to conjure the next stepping stone because the stream, we hope, keeps flowing.[1]

SEAMUS HEANEY, IRISH NOBEL LAUREATE, 1939–2013

OF THE MANY WRITERS who have talked or written about the process of writing, we would expect a poet to provide us with a set of lovely images. Seamus Heaney does not disappoint us. He likens the poet's own poems to stepping stones in a stream. What does the stream symbolize in this analogy?

If you're not surfeited with the topic of stones by this point, use a stone as your central idea to write one or more poems of the following kinds. Rhyme is optional. See Appendix A for sound devices that can substitute for perfect rhyme.

1. Lyden, Seamus Heaney, Dec. 28, 2008.

An Acrostic Poem: a poem in which the first letter of each line of the poem spells a word or words when read from top to bottom. The book of Lamentations contains acrostic poems, but since we are unfamiliar with Hebrew, we'll look at an example in English. Lewis Carroll's poem, "Life is But a Dream," is one well-known example of an acrostic poem; it spells out "ALICE PLEASANCE LIDDELL," the person for whom his *Alice's Adventures in Wonderland* was written (see Appendix B). The word spelled out in your acrostic poem may be as simple as "STONE," or more ambitious such as "TOUCHSTONE" or "IGNEOUS." See the list of research topics in chapter 7 for more word ideas.

A Found Poem: a poem that uses existing bits of writing (literary, journalistic, billboard, food store, online posts, etc.) as the source material for the newfound poem. The key to success is in the choice of found texts (I suggest three), the portions chosen from each text, the arrangement of these snippet texts, and your vision or purpose in creating the found poem. Yes, have a vision. You may change your vision in the process, but there's usually nothing remarkable about unthinkingly throwing random words or texts together. You may add a few of your own words for smoothness and sense, but keep your additions to a minimum. The sources of your original snippets should be cited somewhere, perhaps at the end of the poem.

A Catalogue Verse: a poem that takes the form of a list (also called a list poem) that is unified by its main topic. If you write about stones, you could list types of gems, bits of proverbs or song lyrics about stones, etc. Check the internet for examples of catalogue verse. If you check under "list poems," you'll find many geared toward young children. "Catalogue verse" produces more interesting entries about this ancient poetic form.

A Pantoum: a poem composed of four-line stanzas that follow a pattern of repetition. The second and fourth lines of the first stanza are repeated in the second stanza, where they become the first and third lines of the second stanza. The pattern is continued throughout whatever number of stanzas you decide to write, with the last line of your final stanza repeating the poem's first line. These versification rules often initiate poetic insights or possibilities as you work on forming the poem.

A Concrete Poem: a poem whose textual arrangement visually reveals or comports with the poem's thematic topic. Your text's visual form may resemble an imaginatively shaped stone, or it could resemble the famous Half Dome in California, the eroding Old Man of the Mountain in New Hampshire, or any stone monument or edifice. Fit the poem's thematic content into the image you've chosen as a template for arranging the text. Your line breaks should seem poetically inspired rather than determined only by the outline of the visual item. (See Appendix C)

OTHER CREATIVE WRITING SUGGESTIONS

A Humorous Essay: Contrary to what you might think, a humorous piece of writing is not by nature more superficial than other forms of writing. It requires an eye and ear that sees and hears inconsistences or oddities in human behavior or experience.[2] These become fodder for ironic, satirical or nonsensical treatment. If you stick with the stone motif, you could explore reasons why people do or do not want to have pets, then write your essay about why they might like owning a stone as a pet. You could also treat the Sisyphus myth humorously (maybe . . . it's pretty bleak). When writing a humorous essay, you can relax many of the formal essay writing rules. Your diction may be informal, even slangy.

Your tone is an essential element of your essay's effectiveness. It needn't be smart-alecky or snarky. It might be droll, dry, bemused, rueful, self-deprecatory, or callow. Decide what persona (attitude, stance) you will take toward your subject. Will you be a naïve believer? a shallow sort? a melancholy observer? an envious

2. Four coordinating conjunctions and a prepositional phrase make this sentence a bit clumsy. Care to edit?

acquaintance? Your persona will determine the voice of the piece and drive your tone and the humor.

Screenwriting: One focus of screenwriting is character development, with special emphasis upon characters' words. Actions may speak louder than words, but words speak loudly (even when spoken in hushed tones). Write a brief script for a children's show in which all or some of the characters are stones of various types (pebbles, rocks, diamonds, coal, etc.). Decide whether your primary purpose is education or entertainment. (It may be both, of course!) Refer to the tips on formatting dialogue below.

Short Story (with a focus on setting): Short stories also make use of dialogue and tone, but their effect is sometimes closely tied to their settings. Write a short story set among stones. These could be ancient stones such as those of the Colosseum, the rubble of a war-torn town, or a stone sculpture garden at night. Check the stone research topics suggested in chapter 7 for more ideas.

Short Story (with a focus on plot, theme): The short story format also accommodates plot- or theme-driven writing. Write a story in which a stone is a motif, symbol, or plot element. As a motif or symbol, the stone could be sat upon, stumbled over, or looming in the background. Have in mind the abstract reality symbolized by the stone. As a plot element, the stone might be the object of your characters' search. Or perhaps they are trapped by stones, forced to break rocks in prison, or tasked with clearing stone-filled land in order to plant crops.

In each of these short story possibilities, your details in describing the stone(s) will increase your reader's interest. As someone said, "God is in the details."[3]

TIPS FOR WRITING DIALOGUE

Tip 1: Make it natural and believable.

3. This is one of those quotations that, like its alternate version, "The devil's in the details," has been attributed to several people.

Most films and fiction contain dialogue, and effective dialogue develops characterization, plot, and theme. Give lots of thought (but not necessarily lots of words) to your characters' dialogue. It should suit the character who is speaking (informal or formal diction, vocabulary, idioms, dialect, etc.). It should sound natural and should not merely provide exposition[4] or obvious ties to plot and theme. Look through some of your favorite books for examples of dialogue that memorably "spoke to you." Try to figure out why this dialogue is so effective. Would it work in any time-period? What makes it sound authentic?

Tip 2: The tag
The words that identify the dialogue's speaker are called a tag, and it can precede, interrupt, or follow the dialogue. Pay attention to the punctuation of any tags you write (an example follows below). You do not always need to identify the speaker. It is sometimes obvious, and a stand-alone quotation imitates the flow of natural conversation.

Tip 3: Paragraphing and Punctuation
A new paragraph signals a new speaker. Here's a sample that illustrates the basics of conventional dialogue tags, paragraphing, and punctuation. It includes unspoken interior monologue:

Sylvia burst into the family room and proudly announced, "Grandpa taught me how to skip stones across the lake!" *Her excitement filled the lodge.*

"What?" *Sanford yelled.* "Why didn't he show me how to do that?"

Sylvia's enthusiasm immediately dimmed as she considered her brother's hurt feelings. For a moment, she thought of saying, "Hey, San, don't worry. I'll show you how to do it." *But then she realized that Sanford did not want to learn from her. He wanted the moment with his granddad. So, she said instead,* "Ask him, Sanford. He loves to show people how to do this."

---

4. *Exposition* is background information that is helpful or essential to the story's meaning.

Sanford grumbled a bit more but found himself appeased. "Yeah, okay," he said. "And when I learn how to do it, I'm challenging you to a stone skipping contest!"

"Awesome!"

PICTURE PROMPTS

These are a favorite for creative writers suffering from writer's block. Take a walk—many famous writers have been or are walkers—with your camera to search out your own story-worthy stones, or look through books, magazines, or online. A brief sample of each of the four modes of discourse follows in the next chapter. The descriptive, expository, and narrative examples are based upon this picture:

9

Four Main Modes
of Written Discourse

Chapter 1 briefly defined the four basic modes of discourse. This chapter provides brief examples (and they are *only* examples) of each mode. I've followed each example with annotations explaining my writing choices and identifying rules as well as reasons for bending or ignoring these rules. The example of persuasive writing is based upon interpretations of Robert Frost's poem, "Mending Wall." The other three modes take the picture of the broken stone wall at the end of chapter 8 as their prompt.

DESCRIPTIVE MODE

Fitted within the curve of a clean-swept sidewalk stands a retaining wall fashioned with mortar and asymmetrical stones. Well, much of it remains standing. A small section now lies in defeat and disarray, undone by the persistent push of tree roots from within its boundary. Its smoothed surfaces now face the dirt, revealing jagged irregularities inelegantly clinging to cement gobbets. Crisp, brown, oak leaves stuff the breaches, studding the fallen stones as if to mock the fallen wall with the laurel usually given to the victor.

The part of the wall that still stands is not unmoved. Fissures threaten its broken edges. Once smooth and strong, it now seems sadly vulnerable.

Comments:

1. Every word is important. Avoid the slow starters—expletive constructions such as *there is/are* or articles such as *a* or *the*. Okay, the second paragraph begins with *the*. Can you think of a good change? Be careful not to torture your syntax just to avoid beginning with an article. For instance you wouldn't want to write, "Not unmoved is the still-standing portion." Maybe an additional sentence could begin the paragraph. The addition should preserve the tone and conflict of the piece.

2. "clean-swept sidewalk" is more concise than "The sidewalk is swept clean." It conserves words and keeps the description lean by replacing a five-word sentence with a three-word phrase.

3. The use of *I* (first person point of view) requires words that often bloat a tightly crafted description. Third person works better in descriptive writing, unless the topic being described is oneself. ("Fissures threaten its broken edges" is third person. "I notice fissures in the standing wall" is first person.)

4. Your verbs should be action verbs (*lies, face, stuff, studding, mock,* and *threaten*) rather than linking (*remains*) verbs. You'll notice that I've abandoned this principle in the second paragraph with the linking verbs *is* and *seems*. I wanted a series of short sentences since my first paragraph contains a few long sentences; and linking verbs, which do not express action, emphasize the wall's inability to act in its defense.

5. Your verbs should take the active rather than passive voice unless there is good reason to use passive voice. In active voice, the sentence's subject performs the verb's action ("oak leaves stuff the breaches"). In passive voice, the sentence's

subject receives the verb's action ("the breaches are stuffed with oak leaves"). In this example, active voice belongs to the tree; passive voice expresses the position of the defeated wall. Both perspectives are suitable to the conflict underlying this descriptive piece; therefore, either voice would work to advance the piece's effect.

6. Because my opening sentence is long and formal, I decided to follow it with a short sentence that is informal in tone. Don't overuse this strategy; you don't want to rattle your readers. Vary sentence lengths and types,[1] but don't follow a pattern in your variation (e.g., one long, one short, one long, one short). You don't want to lull your reader into a deep sleep.

7. The word *laurel* is an allusion to a symbol of victory, though the leaves are ironically placed upon the defeated wall section instead of the victorious oak. *Laurel* also plays on the names of trees. The word *unmoved* has a literal and emotional meaning consistent with the piece's martial diction and elegiac[2] tone.

EXPOSITORY MODE

The cause of this wall's partial destruction seems immediately apparent at first—as the oak tree's root system grew, its pressure exceeded the wall's structural ability to retain it. This is an accurate but inadequate explanation of the destructive forces involved. In addition to the physical weathering of root wedging, ice wedging and deicing salts may have contributed to the wall's demise.

This wall is situated in a suburban neighborhood in the Northeastern United States on a heavily trafficked street. In winter, when snow and ice impede travel, city workers salt the streets with spreaders that cast a wide swath. Homeowners also salt their sidewalks to

1. Types of sentences: simple, compound, complex, and compound-complex. See Appendix D.

2. *Elegiac* means sorrowful. As a literary term, an elegy is a poetic tribute to the dead.

make them safe for pedestrians. When these elements reach a wall's foundation, chemical degradation can occur.

Climate certainly contributes to disintegration. The seasonal temperature and precipitation fluctuations in this area of the Northeast are significant. Summer heat and winter cold promote expansion and contraction resulting in ice wedging that breaks down the wall's composition.

Decay and deterioration are facts of life, but the reasons for destruction are varied. In the case of this stone wall, the physical weathering of roots and ice as well as contact with deicing salts may all have contributed to its disintegration.

Comments:

1. Though never the best first word, I began this essay with *the* because the essay's topic is cause(s). The effects of this cause are secondary to this essay's purpose. Even so, an introductory paragraph beginning with effects and ending with causes would work well—perhaps better.

2. I've identified the topic of exposition in the last sentence of my introductory paragraph. This is usually called the thesis sentence, and it can be placed anywhere in the introduction. For instance, I could have begun, "Many degrading forces may have destroyed this wall, though the tree's roots certainly contributed." Place your thesis where it will most effectively inform and interest your reader in the essay's topic.

3. Each body paragraph contains a topic sentence that identifies the point of that paragraph. The topic sentences organize their body paragraphs' support for the essay's thesis. As with the thesis, the topic sentence may be placed anywhere in its paragraph. Have a good reason, though, for its placement. Does its placement increase interest? Does it promote coherence (hanging together)? Try moving sentences around to see how this affects interest, coherence, and comprehension.

4. Notice how the diction and tone of this expository piece differ from that of the descriptive piece. You are not required to adopt a detached, informational tone and analytical diction when writing expositorily, but it suits this topic.

PERSUASIVE MODE

This persuasive mode writing sample requires reading Robert Frost's poem "Mending Wall," which you can find online. Read the poem several times before reading the following essay.

Those of us who have strong opinions about the need for clear property lines might be inclined to agree with the neighbor in Robert Frost's poem "Mending Wall," who twice asserts that "good fences make good neighbours." Many have quoted this line as a statement of the poem's theme. This interpretation misses ironic shifts in diction and tone, however, that support the speaker's twice-uttered contrary assertion: "something there is that doesn't love a wall." Despite evidence of the two men's initial collaborative unity in maintaining the wall, the poem ultimately criticizes the structure as a useless and even offensive barrier and those who maintain it as slaves to worn-out traditions.

Both the speaker and his neighbor seem amicably engaged in the wall-mending at first. They meet at the speaker's suggestion (line 12), and the speaker refers to their work as an "out-door game" (line 21). They jokingly invoke a magic spell to prevent the replaced boulders from falling off again, "until our backs are turned!" (line19). Their camaraderie is evident in the plural personal pronouns—six "we" and three "us"—that dot the first half of the poem.

These pronouns disappear and are replaced by the singular pronouns "he," "I," "me," and "him" in the last half of the poem. The shift occurs after the speaker questions his neighbor's assertion that "good fences make good neighbours" (line 27). Still in a playful mood, he mischievously wonders if he "could put a notion in his head," and asks,

"Why do they make good neighbours? Isn't it

Where there are cows? But here there are no cows.
Before I built a wall I'd ask to know
What I was walling in or walling out,
And to whom I was like to give offense.
Something there is that doesn't love a wall,
That wants it down." (lines 30–36)

It is a reasonable question, aimed at discerning a rationale for common assumptions and past practices. The neighbor, intent upon completing the ritual, makes no reply other than to simply repeat his earlier claim that "good fences make good neighbours." This second instance ends the poem.

In giving the neighbor the literal last word, Frost may seem to be giving him the thematic final word, but the context preceding this last line argues for a different reading. The speaker seems irked by his neighbor's refusal to engage in debate ("I'd rather / He said it for himself.") The next line observes that in "bringing a stone grasped firmly by the top / In each hand" (lines 39–40), his neighbor resembles "an old-stone savage armed" who "moves in darkness as it seems to me / Not of woods only and the shade of trees" (lines 40–42). Then, in the two lines leading up to the neighbor's closing statement, the speaker practically spits his growing contempt for him and his timeworn hereditary maxim:

He will not go behind his father's saying
And he likes having thought of it so well
He says again, "Good fences make good neighbours." (lines 43–45)

The poem's irony is evident in its title, in the neighbor's assertion, and the speaker's own assertion, which opens the poem. Their juxtaposed claims imply a clear debate, but the neighbor is uninterested in this intellectual activity, and the speaker's internal monologue encourages the reader to agree that the neighbor is benighted ("He moves in darkness"), simple ("he likes having thought of it so well"), and a slave to tradition ("He will not go behind his father's saying").

Much more than a fence is needed, the poem implies, to make people with different perspectives into good neighbors. The mundane *ritual that unites two men in a joint mending task exposes a philosophical barrier that has also been strengthened in the process. Ironically, the wall-mending venture results in the dismantling of any previously existing goodwill between these neighbors.*

Comments:

1. Forgive this pun: the boundary between persuasive and expository essays of the compare and contrast kind is sometimes difficult to discern. A poem analysis by itself is rarely the subject of a persuasive or argumentative essay. This particular poem, however, presents its own internal set of contrasting opinions, making it especially suitable to a persuasive essay about contrasting interpretive understandings. Had I referenced sources whose interpretations differ significantly from the one I propose, this sample would better illustrate an argumentative or persuasive writing. Nonetheless, the framework of this essay provides an overview for writing a persuasive piece.

2. A basic rule for persuasive writing is that the introductory paragraph should identify a conflict, opposing viewpoints, and a position in favor of one over the other(s).

3. Your body paragraphs work to elaborate upon these identifications (conflict, opposing viewpoints, and favored position).

4. Do not mistake the poem's speaker or narrator for the poet. Though the speaker may express the poet's point of view, he may just as easily voice a counter-opinion (as in the case of dramatic monologue or dramatic irony.) As clumsy as it sometimes sounds, lacking a name, you must refer to the one speaking as "the speaker." In the fourth paragraph, however, I refer to Frost because I am referring to the writer of the poem rather than the person or character in the poem.

5. There is so much more that could be written about this poem and much that could be written differently. For instance, a different persuasive thesis might focus on the speaker's

hateful characterization of his neighbor—an ironic contrast to his professed aversion to giving offense (line 34)—and the fact that he allows him no fuller perspective of his own in this fence-mending project.

6. I've placed my line citations in parentheses. This illustrates MLA Style Manual preference.

NARRATIVE MODE

With a good deal of trepidation, I had decided to fly 1800 miles to attend my high school's twentieth reunion. A twentieth reunion has heft. It isn't a fiftieth, but enough time has elapsed to distinguish it from, say, a tenth.

The dread we experience about such reunions seems to flow from our inexhaustible wrestle with Time. We know that Time has altered our faces, hair volume, and physical sprightliness. We know that Time has measured our use of it—some of our classmates will have professional and personal achievements that we'll applaud even as we simultaneously self-flagellate.

Despite this trepidation, I looked forward to planting my feet on the soil of those formative years. I would soon walk again among the streets, houses, playgrounds, and alleys that were the mise en scène³ of my youth; and I would revel in my transport.

Now as I walked those paths of my past, the reverie of memory was extinguished by my glimpse of the familiar retaining wall just ahead. It was a landmark in my daily walk to and from school— solid, reliable, and permanent. There it stood as a ruin, its former solidity broken now into bits of stone, mortar, and leafy mold.

Time did not intrude upon the reunion; Time was an unavoid-able guest. Our bodies, lives, and memories, healthy and happy at present, could not escape Time's presence. Time folded testimonies of blight and ruin into our reunion—into our enjoyment of things solid, reliable, and permanent.

3. *Mise en scène*: a theatrical term for the placement of items on a stage. This placement contributes toward the theme of the play or movie.

Comments:

1. First words and first sentences are crucial to engaging your reader. I began with a phrase about trepidation, because fear interests most of us, and because there's some ambiguity in the first sentence about whether the fear concerns flying or the reunion.

2. I've chosen first person point of view. Would this work in third person?

3. The second paragraph identifies its audience. Details such as aging bodies and professional achievements mostly interest people over a certain age. A word like *self-flagellate*, which means to strike oneself with a whip, may not be known to those who haven't read about this medieval religious practice. *Mise en scène* may be known to high school drama students, but it's a technical term. Know your audience. For whom are you writing this piece? Consider age, gender, culture, level of education, religious or political beliefs, occupation, etc. Tailor your writing to your intended audience, but do not condescend or rely on stereotyped generalities.

4. The final paragraph of my narrative, with its personification and allegoric language, bears a strong resemblance to Edgar A. Poe's allegorical story, "The Masque of the Red Death," though mine is not nearly as macabre. Poe's story is written in third person point of view, which is of especial interest given his apocalyptic theme. I might be accused of plagiarism in my final paragraph were it not for the fact that the theme of Time's effect on human experience is widespread in literature. Some will point out that all literature draws from previous literary sources—Poe's story draws from and alludes to Biblical and extra-Biblical material—and they are quite pleased to bring William Shakespeare in as "Exhibit A" in this discussion. With so much to be said about this, I will only suggest that you read some authors who are commonly referred to as classical writers. This will equip you to better avoid hackneyed themes. (You may also want to look up the literary definitions of *homage* and *parody*.)

Appendix A

Sᴏᴜɴᴅ ɪs ᴀ ᴘᴏᴡᴇʀғᴜʟ aspect of a word's connotation. *Maelstrom*, for me, was both visually and aurally resonant. Treat words as living entities and not as lifeless stones. What follows is a brief taxonomy of sound devices.

Perfect Rhyme: We are most familiar with easy-to-hear rhymes such as *rain/stain, apple/grapple, home/roam, laughter/after*, etc. The words are identical in sound and in the number and stress of syllables.

Assonance: While not a perfect rhyme, assonant words are placed near each other (or at end of lines), and they share a vowel sound. It must be a vowel sound; not all vowels share the same sound.[1] Examples of assonance include *paper/staple, move/stoop, stand/plan*, and *ice/time*. Assonance is sometimes called imperfect rhyme or slant rhyme.

Consonance: This definition is similar to the definition for assonance, but it applies to consonants rather than vowels. A similar consonant sound repeats among words in close proximity (or in words at end of lines). Examples of consonance include *bitter/throttle, reproach/approve*, and *bumble/able*. The repeated consonant sounds can occur anywhere in the words—beginning, middle, or end. Consonance is also sometimes called imperfect rhyme.

1. For instance, *bid* and *bide*, or *bid* and *tight* share the same *i* vowel, but not the same vowel sound.

Alliteration: Alliteration is sometimes confused with consonance because it also involves consonants. Alliteration is a specialized form of consonance because the repeated consonant sounds must be found in the first stressed syllable. Most often, alliteration occurs in the first letters of successive words. Examples of alliteration include <u>s</u>eepage/<u>s</u>almon, <u>st</u>erile/<u>st</u>riking, <u>c</u>ease/<u>s</u>ilt, jumbo/gentle, and <u>br</u>isk/<u>br</u>eeze.

Appendix B

"Life is But a Dream" or "A Boat Beneath a Sunny Sky"
L EWIS C ARROLL

A boat, beneath a sunny sky
Lingering onward dreamily
In an evening of July—

Children three that nestle near,
Eager eye and willing ear,
Pleased a simple tale to hear—

Long has paled that sunny sky:
Echoes fade and memories die:
Autumn frosts have slain July.

Still she haunts me, phantomwise,
Alice moving under skies
Never seen by waking eyes.

Children yet, the tale to hear,
Eager eye and willing ear,
Lovingly shall nestle near.

In a Wonderland they lie,
Dreaming as the days go by,
Dreaming as the summers die:

Ever drifting down the stream—
Lingering in the golden gleam—
Life, what is it but a dream?

Appendix C

"This Crosstree Here"

<small>Robert Herrick</small>

> This crosstree here
> Doth Jesus bear,
> Who sweet'ned first,
> The death accurs'd.
> HERE all things ready are, make haste, make haste away;
> For long this work will be and very short this day.
> Why then, go on to act: here's wonders to be done
> Before the last least sand of Thy ninth hour be run;
> Or ere dark clouds do dull or dead the mid-day's sun.
> Act when Thou wilt,
> Blood will be spilt;
> Pure balm, that shall
> Bring health to all.
> Why then, begin
> To pour first in
> Some drops of wine,
> Instead of brine,
> To search the wound
> So long unsound:
> And, when that's done,

Let oil next run
To cure the sore
Sin made before.
And O! dear Christ,
E'en as Thou di'st,
Look down, and see
Us weep for Thee.
And tho', love knows,
Thy dreadful woes
We cannot ease,
Yet do Thou please,
Who mercy art,
T' accept each heart
That gladly would
Help if it could.
Meanwhile let me,
Beneath this tree,
This honour have,
To make my grave.

Appendix D

IT'S EASY TO IMAGINE the demise of the following classifications. They may one day be replaced by descriptive[1] rather than prescriptive models. Even so, familiarity with formal conventions encourages reasoned discussion about proposed changes when they occur.[2] What follows are conventional definitions and examples of sentence types. Subjects of clauses are underlined once; verbs are underlined twice.

Clause: a group of words containing a subject and a predicate.

Dependent clauses cannot stand alone; they are dependent upon the *independent clause* to form a complete sentence. In the examples below, "though he spent a lifetime searching for it," "who is a stone mason," and "that they are up to code" are dependent clauses.

Phrase: two or more words lacking a subject and its predicate. In the examples below, "in the vast desert," "According to Hilda's grandfather," and "up to code" are phrases.

---

1. In this usage, *descriptive* describes the way language is used. *Prescriptive* prescribes the way language should be used, according to those conversant with the history and logic of linguistics.

2. Perhaps you've noticed that I've used contractions and begun sentences with conjunctions in this book. These transgressions of formal grammar are increasingly (but not unanimously) acceptable.

- A *Simple* sentence has only one clause with one subject and one predicate.

  The large, jagged stone was *a striking sight in the vast desert.* (The predicate includes the verb *was*, which is a linking verb, and the words that follow.)

  According to Hilda's grandfather, the outside fireplace had been hewn *from a tremendous stone.* (The verb phrase *had been hewn* is an example of passive voice. In order to change it to active voice, we would have to know who did the hewing.)

- A *Compound* sentence has two or more independent clauses and no dependent clauses.

  He spent *a lifetime searching for it, but* he *never* discovered *the Philosopher's Stone.* (When joining two independent clauses, use a semicolon, or use a coordinating conjunction—*and, but, or, nor, for, so, yet*—preceded by a comma. The words *not* and *never* are never part of the verb. In this sentence, *searching* is a participle not a verb.)

- A *Complex* sentence has one independent clause and one or more dependent clauses.

  Though he spent *a lifetime searching for it,* he *never* discovered *the Philosopher's Stone.* (*Though he spent a lifetime searching for it* cannot stand alone because it is introduced by a subordinating conjunction, *though*.)

- A *Compound-Complex* sentence has at least two independent clauses and one or more dependent clauses.

  My neighbor, who is *a stone mason,* evaluated *the condition of my steps, and* he said *that* they are *up to code.* (This sentence comprises two independent clauses and two dependent clauses. *who is a stone mason* is an adjective clause introduced by the relative pronoun *who*. It is a dependent clause. If it were intended as a question, *Who is a stone mason?* it would be an independent clause because *who* in this use is a pronoun, not a relative pronoun. The parts of speech of many words are determined by their use in the phrase or sentence. This, too, is a matter of context!)

Bibliography

The Concise Oxford Dictionary of English Etymology, ed. T.F. Hoad, Oxford: Clarendon, 1986.

Cresswell, Julia, ed. *Oxford Dictionary of Word Origins*, Oxford University Press, 2010.

Davis, John D. "stone" in *Davis Dictionary of the Bible*. 4th revised ed. Michigan: Baker Book House, 1975.

Heaney, Seamus. Interview by Jacki Lyden, *All Things Considered*, NPR, Dec. 28, 2008.

Moules, Nancy J. "Hermeneutic Inquiry: Paying Heed to History and Hermes An Ancestral, Substantive, and Methodological Tale." *International Journal of Qualitative Methods*, (September 2002) 1–21. doi:10.1177/160940690200100301.

Trumble, William, and Martin Brown, eds. *The Shorter Oxford English Dictionary: On Historical Principles*, 5th ed. vol. 1, Oxford: Oxford University Press, 2002.

"The Westminster Confession of Faith" in *Trinity Hymnal*. revised ed., Philadelphia: Great Commission, 1990.